Earth: The Water Planet

by E.C. Hill

Table of Contents

Pictures To Think About

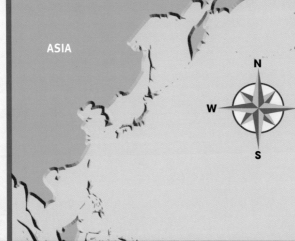

ARCTIC
OCEAN

NORTH
AMERICA

ASIA

PACIFIC
OCEAN

Earth: The Water Planet

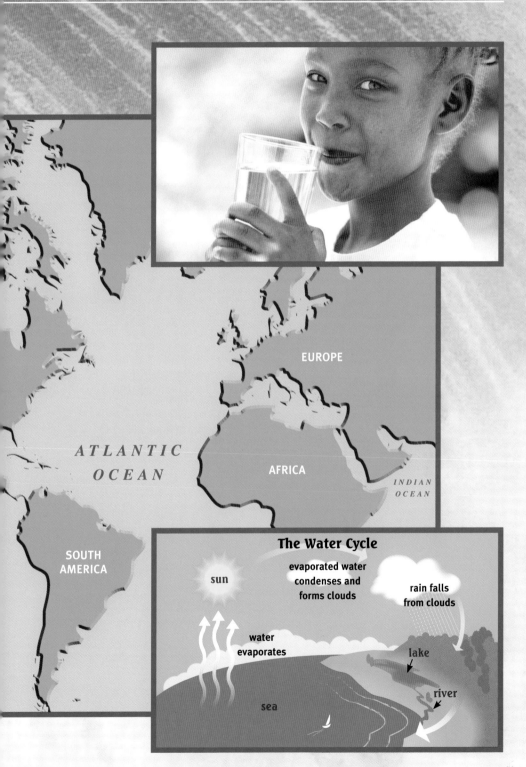

EUROPE

ATLANTIC
OCEAN

AFRICA

INDIAN
OCEAN

SOUTH
AMERICA

The Water Cycle

evaporated water
condenses and
forms clouds

rain falls
from clouds

sun

water
evaporates

lake

river

sea

Words To Think About

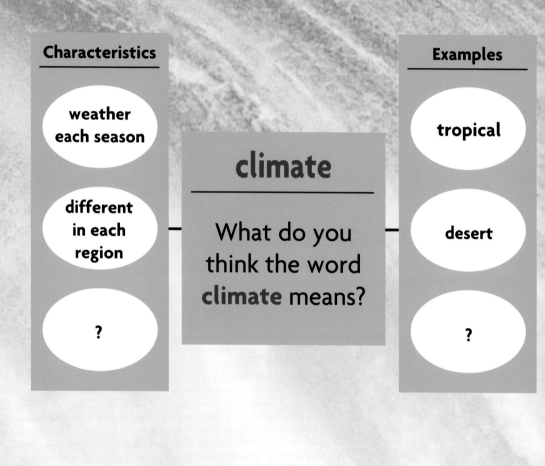

Characteristics

- weather each season
- different in each region
- ?

climate

What do you think the word **climate** means?

Examples

- tropical
- desert
- ?

aquifer

Latin: *aqua* (water)

What do you think the word **aquifer** means?

Latin: *fer* (to carry or bring)

Read for More Clues

aquifer, page 22
climate, page 3
spring, page 19

spring

What do you think the word **spring** means in this book?

Meaning 1
to leap
or jump
(verb)

Meaning 2
season
of the year
(noun)

Meaning 3
a place where
water comes
from underground
(noun)

iv

Introduction

All living things need water to live. You do, too. Your body is made mostly of water. More than 65% of the human body is water.

Water is everywhere. You can find water in many places on Earth. If you were in space looking at Earth, you'd see mostly water.

▲ This watering hole is in Etosha National Park, Namibia.

Read this book to learn more about water. Learn how oceans affect the world's **climate** (KLY-mut). Find out where water comes from and how we use it.

Oceans

Water covers most of Earth. Most of that water is in the oceans. Earth has five oceans. They are the Pacific, Atlantic, Indian, Southern, and Arctic oceans.

Ocean water has salt. **Salinity** (sah-LIH-nih-tee) is how much salt is in water. Ocean water has about 3.5% salt. You can taste the salt in ocean water.

They Made a Difference

Otis Barton and William Beebe were the first people to go down to the deepest parts of the ocean. The two men designed the first bathysphere to take them into the deep sea. It looked like a steel ball with a window in it. The two men used it to dive over 3,000 feet (914 meters) down into the ocean. A 400-pound (181-kilogram) door locked it tight.

The Pacific Ocean is approximately what fraction of the world's oceans? Hint: This is a two-step problem. First you have to add together all the oceans. You can estimate to get an approximate answer.

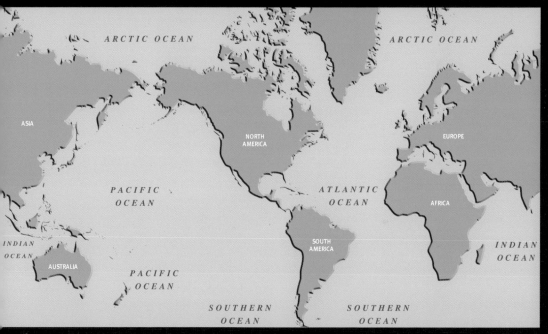

▲ Over 70% of Earth's surface is covered by water.

Oceans

Ocean	Size
Pacific Ocean	60,060,893 sq mi (155,557,000 sq km)
Atlantic Ocean	29,637,974 sq mi (76,762,000 sq km)
Indian Ocean	26,469,620 sq mi (68,556,000 sq km)
Southern Ocean	7,848,299 sq mi (20,327,000 sq km)
Arctic Ocean	5,427,052 sq mi (14,056,000 sq km)

The Ocean Floor

The ocean floor has mountains, valleys, hills, and plains.
We can't see these features. They are under the water.
Let's look under the water. Let's look at the ocean floor.

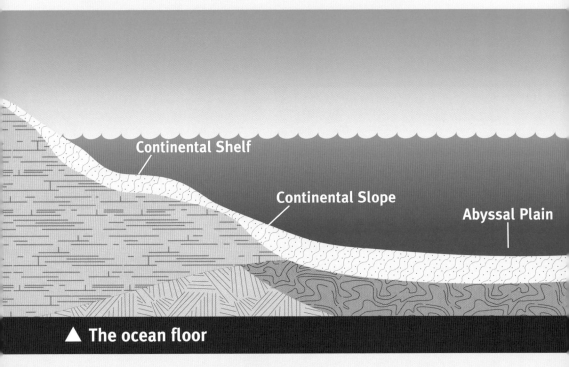

Continental Shelf

Continental Slope

Abyssal Plain

▲ The ocean floor

It's a Fact

The highest point on Earth is Mount Everest. The lowest point in the oceans is in the Marianas Trench in the Pacific Ocean. The longest mountain range is in the ocean. It's called the mid-ocean ridge. It runs for more than 50,000 miles (80,467.2 kilometers). Scientists now know that the mid-ocean ridge is part of every ocean on Earth.

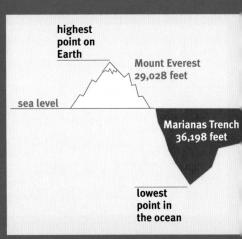

highest point on Earth

Mount Everest 29,028 feet

sea level

Marianas Trench 36,198 feet

lowest point in the ocean

The ocean floor has three parts. One part is the **continental shelf** (kahn-tih-NEN-tul SHELF). This part surrounds the edges of a continent. A continent is a large mass of land.

The next part is the **continental slope** (kahn-tih-NEN-tul SLOPE). Here the ocean floor drops down steeply.

The continental slope goes very deep very fast. Then the ocean floor becomes flat. This flat part is the **abyssal plain** (uh-BIH-sul PLANE). The abyssal plain covers almost one-half of Earth's surface.

▲ Have you ever been to an ocean beach? When you walked into the water, you were on the continental shelf.

7

Oceans on the Move

Have you ever watched ocean waves roll in toward the shore? The water in the ocean is always moving. What makes ocean water move?

First, the sun heats the air over the ocean. Warm air is lighter than cold air. The warm air rises. Then cooler air flows in to replace the warm air. This makes wind. Whoosh!

Wind blowing on the surface of the ocean pushes the water. This push piles the water into waves. The harder the wind blows, the bigger the waves.

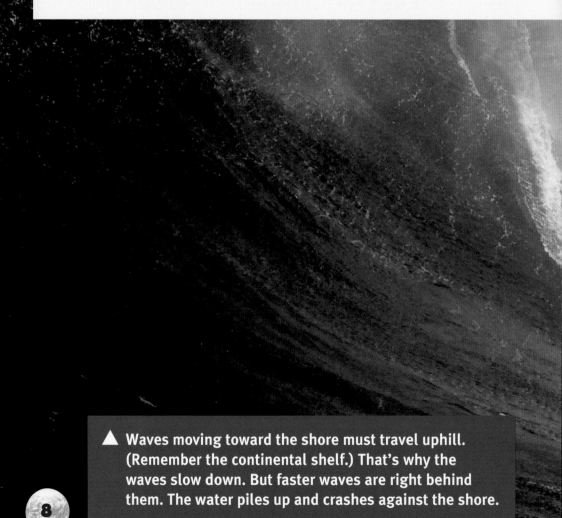

▲ Waves moving toward the shore must travel uphill. (Remember the continental shelf.) That's why the waves slow down. But faster waves are right behind them. The water piles up and crashes against the shore.

Everyday Science

Ocean water contains many minerals. But the main mineral is sodium chloride. That's the same salt people put on food.

Currents

Wind blows over the ocean day after day. During the day, wind blows from the water to the land. At night, the wind blows the opposite way.

Wind makes the water move in strong currents. An ocean current is like a river that flows through the ocean.

Currents flow in all oceans. Currents carry cold water to warm places. They also carry warm water to cold places. Some currents move in circles.

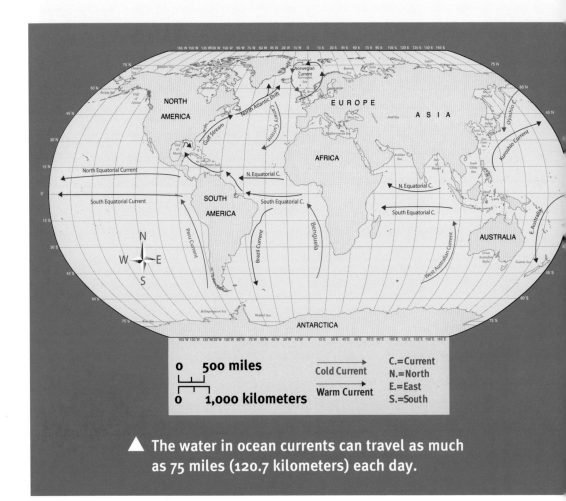

▲ The water in ocean currents can travel as much as 75 miles (120.7 kilometers) each day.

The Gulf Stream is a large ocean current. The Gulf Stream starts in the warm waters near Florida. Then it moves northeast in the Atlantic Ocean. It brings warm water to northwestern Europe. The Gulf Stream warms the climate there. Northwestern Europe would be much colder without the Gulf Stream.

It's a Fact

Benjamin Franklin discovered that the fastest way to sail from America to England was to use the Gulf Stream. His discovery sped up the delivery of mail between America and Great Britain.

▲ Palm trees grow along the southwest coast of Great Britain. The Gulf Stream warms this area enough for palm trees to grow here.

Weather and the Water Cycle

It is a hot day. You swim in a pool. You get out and walk to your towel. You leave wet footprints as you walk. In a minute your footprints are gone. Where did they go?

Heat made the water **evaporate** (ih-VA-puh-rate). Liquids such as water change to **vapor** (VAY-per), or gas, when they evaporate. The water in your footprints changed to gas and floated away.

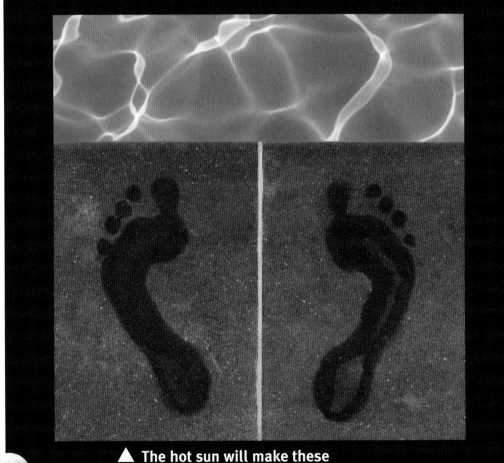

▲ The hot sun will make these wet footprints evaporate quickly.

The same thing happens with oceans and other bodies of water. The sun heats the water. Then a lot of water evaporates. The vapor rises into the air.

The vapor cools high in the sky. It **condenses** (kun-DENS-is), or changes from a gas into a liquid. The tiny drops of liquid water collect in the air. Clouds form from these tiny drops.

When the drops become too heavy, water falls from the clouds. Often this water falls as rain.

The Water Cycle

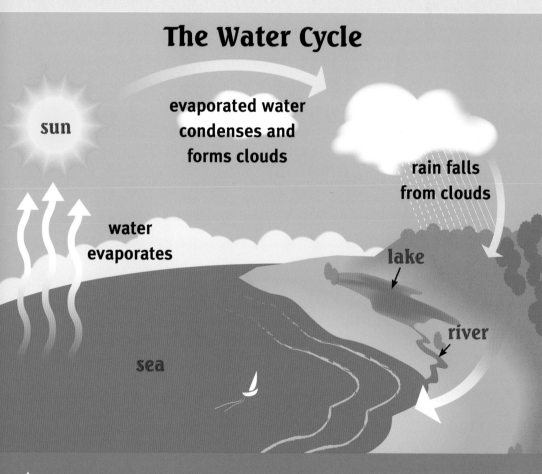

sun

evaporated water condenses and forms clouds

rain falls from clouds

water evaporates

lake

river

sea

▲ Water evaporates from lakes, rivers, and other bodies of water. However, nearly 80% of all evaporation is from the oceans.

Some places get lots of rain. Wind and rain follow patterns. A pattern does the same thing each time.

One wind pattern is a **monsoon** (mahn-SOON). Monsoons affect India. They also affect other parts of Asia.

Monsoons happen in summer. The sun is hot. Strong winds blow over the Indian Ocean. Moist air from the ocean forms clouds over the land. Then heavy rain falls.

▲ Some of the wettest places on Earth are in India. Some areas get over 400 inches (1,016 centimeters) of rain in an average year.

Clouds and the Wind

Clouds are almost always moving. Wind moves the clouds. Remember that clouds are full of water. When clouds move, water moves too.

Sometimes the water stays in the clouds for days. Other times the water falls as rain. The water can also fall as snow, sleet, or hail.

▲ Clouds cover about 60% of the sky at any time.

✔ Point

Make Connections

What other fiction or nonfiction books have you read about clouds? How was the information the same as or different from what you read in this book?

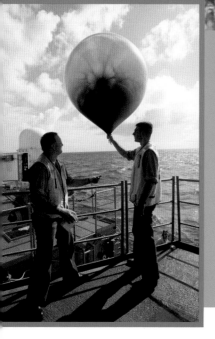

Careers in Science

Do you wonder why different locations have different climates? Then being a climatologist might be the job for you. Climatologists are scientists who study the average weather conditions over a long period of time. One of their jobs is to gather information about the causes of weather patterns. Climatologists are worried that Earth's climate is changing in dramatic ways.

Completing the Water Cycle

The sun gives off heat. Heat energy moves water around the planet. A force moves water, too. This force is **gravity** (GRA-vih-tee). Gravity pulls objects toward the center of Earth. Gravity pulls rain from clouds to the ground.

It's a Fact

The amount of water in the planet's water cycle never changes. The water that falls as rain or snow has existed for billions of years. It has moved through the water cycle countless times.

▲ Storms, like hurricanes, carry large amounts of water from the sea to the land.

16

Most rain sinks into the ground. Sometimes there is too much rain. The extra water becomes **runoff** (RUN-auf). Runoff flows over the land. It may reach streams and rivers.

Gravity pulls the water in streams and rivers downhill. Many rivers flow into oceans. When the water reaches the ocean, the water cycle is complete. Then the cycle starts all over again.

✔ **Point**

Reread

Reread page 13 to find out where the water in clouds comes from.

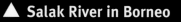
▲ **Salak River in Borneo**

Fresh Water

The water we drink is fresh water. Fresh water is not salty. When water evaporates from the ocean, the salt stays behind. Water vapor is pure water. This pure water makes clouds. Rain water is fresh water.

Lakes hold fresh water. Lakes are bodies of water surrounded by land. Ponds hold fresh water, too. Ponds are smaller than lakes.

▲ There are millions of lakes in the world. Canada alone has about two million.

Water from streams and rivers may flow into lakes and ponds. Water also goes in lakes from **springs** (SPRINGZ). Springs are places where water flows up from underground.

Lake Superior is the largest lake in the world. Lake Baikal in Asia is not as wide as Lake Superior. But Lake Baikal holds more fresh water than Lake Superior. This is because Lake Baikal is the deepest lake in the world.

Lake	Depth
Superior	1,333 feet (406 meters)
Baikal	5,370 feet (1,637 meters)

▲ Lake Superior is the deepest of the Great Lakes at over 1,300 feet (396.2 meters) deep. Lake Baikal is about four times as deep.

It's a Fact

Every living thing needs water to survive. Most animals are mostly made of water. Plants also contain plenty of water. Even the driest plants are about 50% water.

Rivers

Rivers are different from lakes. Lakes hold water. Rivers move water. Water flows downhill in rivers.

Many rivers start high in the mountains. Often they start as streams. Streams rush downhill from the high ground. When many streams come together, they become a river.

▲ Yangtze River

2. Solve This

How much longer is the Nile River than the Yangtze River?

The World's Longest Rivers	
River	Length
Nile (Africa)	4,100 miles (6,598.3 km)
Amazon (South America)	4,000 miles (6,437.4 km)
Mississippi/Missouri (North America)	3,800 miles (6,115.5 km)
Yangtze (Asia)	3,700 miles (5,954.6 km)
Yenisei (Asia)	3,400 miles (5,471.8 km)

The Amazon River is in South America. The Amazon is one of the longest rivers in the world. The Amazon starts as a small stream high in the Andes Mountains. The stream moves very fast downhill.

Other streams join it. Together the streams become larger and larger. More than 1,000 streams pour water into the Amazon. That is why the Amazon is such a mighty river.

✔ Point

Visualize

Use the information on this page to draw what you think the Amazon looks like at its beginning.

▲ The Amazon River holds nearly one-fifth of the river water in the world.

Underground Water and Ice Caps

You can find fresh water in two other places. Each of these places holds more fresh water than all the lakes and rivers combined.

The first place is under the ground. Rain water sinks into the ground. Some of the water passes deep into the layers of sand and rock. That water builds up after thousands of years. Huge amounts of water are underground. The underground layers that hold fresh water are called **aquifers** (A-kwih-ferz).

▲ The Ogallala Aquifer is an important source of underground water. It's found under the Great Plains of the United States.

You can also find fresh water in very cold places. Ice is a form of fresh water. Places such as Antarctica and Greenland are covered in layers of ice. These layers of ice are called **ice caps** (ISE KAPS). Ice caps form when snow builds up. Over time, the snow becomes packed into layers of ice.

The ice caps in Antarctica are nearly 3 miles (4.8 kilometers) thick in places. Some of this ice may be over 400,000 years old.

▲ Glaciers form the same way ice caps do. Many glaciers are found in high mountains, where snow builds up over time.

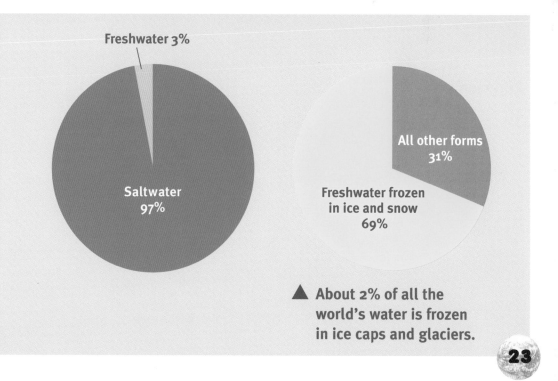

Freshwater 3%

Saltwater 97%

All other forms 31%

Freshwater frozen in ice and snow 69%

▲ About 2% of all the world's water is frozen in ice caps and glaciers.

23

Using Water

You use water every day. You drink water. You wash with water. Your family cooks with water.

Farmers use water to grow food. Farmers also give water to the animals they raise.

It's a Fact

Americans are lucky to have a large supply of water in most areas of the country. People in the United States use a great deal, too. For inside uses, like drinking, cooking, and washing, Americans use seventy-four gallons of water per person every day.

3. Solve This

In which of the ways do Americans use the most water? Which use is just over 1/5 of the total?

How Do Americans Use Water?

Kitchen 5%

Cleaning (washing machines, etc.) 21%

Bathroom 74%

When you turn on a light, you may be using water. Dams on rivers can make electricity. The dams use machines called **turbines** (TER-binez). Turbines use the flow of water to make electricity.

Water has another important use. Water is also fun! Many people enjoy fishing, swimming, and boating in water.

▲ Millions enjoy lakes in the summer. Some even fish on frozen lakes in the winter.

▲ Rivers flowing into Canada's Hudson Bay are dammed to produce electricity.

Overuse

People do not always use water wisely. People in cities use a lot of water. After the water is used, the water is dirty. The dirty water is called wastewater.

In the past, cities moved their wastewater into rivers or oceans. Today, many cities clean their wastewater before they release it.

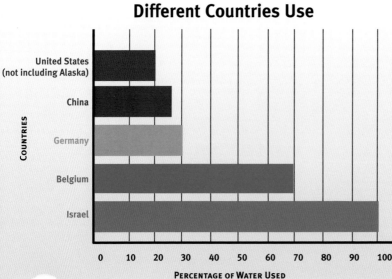

The Amount of Water Different Countries Use

Countries / Percentage of Water Used

- United States (not including Alaska)
- China
- Germany
- Belgium
- Israel

0 10 20 30 40 50 60 70 80 90 100

◄ Israel has a dry climate. That's why it uses all the available fresh water to meet its needs.

Water can be overused. Water from deep underground is pumped to the surface. Farmers in the United States use this water every day. Rain replaces the water but it takes a long time. Wells can go dry when too much water is used too quickly.

The Aral Sea

▲ The Aral Sea in central Asia was once the fourth largest lake in the world. Much of the water in the rivers that fed the lake was taken away for farming and other purposes. The sea has shrunk and split into several smaller lakes. Scientists worry that it may disappear completely in the future.

Water and the Future

The world's population is growing fast. More and more people will need to use fresh, clean water.

Water is a limited resource. A resource is something that is valuable. The amount of fresh water on Earth is not growing. How can people meet their needs?

It's a Fact

The Florida Everglades are natural wetlands. They once covered more than four million acres. Today they cover only half that much land. But people are buying back land that was turned into farms. They plan to make the land part of the Everglades again.

Wetlands are one answer. These low, marshy areas make water cleaner. Wetlands filter waste from water. Some towns have built wetlands to treat wastewater.

Wetlands are also homes for many plants and animals. People can visit wetlands to enjoy nature.

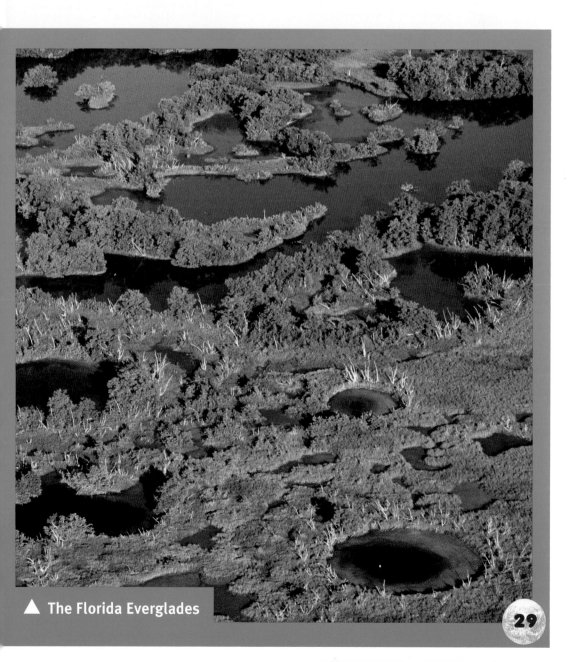

▲ The Florida Everglades

Conclusion

Earth holds a lot of water. Most of this water is in the oceans. The oceans have salt water. The water evaporates and forms clouds. Rain and snow fall from clouds.

Rain and snow bring fresh water to the land. Lakes and rivers have fresh water. Fresh water is also found underground and in ice caps.

People use fresh water for drinking, washing, and growing food. People cannot live without water.

Water is a limited resource. People must use water wisely.

Water	
Salt water	in oceans
Fresh water	in lakes, rivers, aquifers, and ice
People use water	in many ways

Glossary

abyssal plain (uh-BIH-sul PLANE) the vast floor of the deep ocean (page 7)

aquifer (A-kwih-fer) an underground layer of sand, gravel, or stone that contains water (page 22)

climate (KLY-mut) the average weather conditions of a place or region throughout the year (page 3)

condenses (kun-DENS-is) changes from a gas to a liquid upon cooling (page 13)

continental shelf (kahn-tih-NEN-tul SHELF) the gently sloping part of a continent that is under water (page 7)

continental slope (kahn-tih-NEN-tul SLOPE) the edge of a continent that drops steeply down to the deep ocean floor (page 7)

evaporate (ih-VA-puh-rate) to become a vapor, or gas (page 12)

gravity (GRA-vih-tee) the force that pulls objects toward the center of Earth (page 16)

ice cap (ISE KAP) a thick layer of permanent ice (page 23)

monsoon (mahn-SOON) a pattern of wind and rain in the Indian Ocean and southern Asia (page 14)

runoff (RUN-auf) rain that flows over the ground and into streams (page 17)

salinity (sah-LIH-nih-tee) saltiness (page 4)

spring (SPRING) a place where underground water flows to the surface (page 19)

turbine (TER-bine) a machine that uses the power of flowing water to make electricity (page 25)

vapor (VAY-per) The gaseous state of matter (page 12)

Answers to Solve This

Page 5: about 46% **Page 24:** bathroom; cleaning
Page 20: 400 miles (643.7 km)

Index